GODS OF UNFINISHED BUSINESS

Poems on History
Transformed into Myth

Nina Kossman

Foreword by Ilya Kaminsky

Červená Barva Press
Somerville, Massachusetts

Červená Barva Press
USPS P. O. Box 53
Somerville, MA 02143

editor@cervenabarvapress.com
http://www.cervenabarvapress.com

Visit the bookstore at:
http://www.thelostbookshelf.com

Production: Allison O'Keefe
Cover art by Nina Kossman
Cover design: David Ter-Avanesyan/Ter33Design LLC

ISBN: 978-1-950063-64-2
LCCN: 2025945287

Contents

GODS OF UNFINISHED BUSINESS

Poems on History
Transformed into Myth

On Nina Kossman's Histories and Myths

Foreword by Ilya Kaminsky

What is Nina Kossman's God, and what kind of Unfinished Business are we about to get into, I wondered, opening this book of poems. "History Transformed into Myth," the subtitle at the front of these pages warned, and I wondered what is history if not already a myth.

That's what I thought, getting started, yes—right before I learned that Kossman sent me these poems from a warzone, literally: the poet's e-mail said she was in the occupied Ukraine at that time. And just like that, the mythological history, whatever that is, became a documentary fact.

Facts take an interesting role in this collection of poems, actually: we begin with an echo of an ancient Akkadian text also taking place in a warzone, though of a very different kind. And, indeed, the myth comes forth. Or, rather, the myth is denied us ("What Ismul's soul learned in the city of souls is never revealed") only to be revealed as the pages turn:

> "When Ismul's soul flew close to Ismul's body,
> it poured pity over his limbs and chest,
> and it opened Ismul's mouth and poured the rest
>   down his throat.
>
> And only when Ismul's body was drenched in pity,
> was Ismul's soul ready to re-enter the young man's flesh.
> Then Ismul arose from the field of battle
> and went off by himself, only gods know where.
> His army of ragged young men came to him

from every corner of the Amkabadian land.
And when they were gone, rumors were heard of them,
they were said to be seen here and there,
without their swords and shields, yet untouched
by an enemy weapon. Heroes! Heroes of a different sort!
And where they passed, the land became fertile.

This lyric dream of swords transformed to ploughshares comes to us from times immemorial, even Plato, that enemy of poets, longs for it at the end of his *Republic* when Er, the warrior hero of a warrior culture dies, and in his eternal life, the underworld, chooses not to be a hero, chooses the life of an ordinary man.

Years pass—Nina Kossman is the first to remind us of that, it is the "second decade of a third millennium," she writes, and yet the old myths reverberate, albeit transformed by the present. And if we see how "Helen's shadow on Trojan rocks / still threatens the Greeks," it is because it burdens them "with the highest taxes," an irony that doesn't escape the readers of these pages, who too might find themselves whispering the poems in this or that "middle-class teashop" while on TV "machines count the killed" and it is that time of the year when "spring, a fruitless autumn, / quiet markets."

If you overhear the ironic note here, you aren't alone. But then you are also not alone to look in the streets of your cities and notice how "the wretched pass for the mad, / the mad for licentious" while the rest of us are "washed clean of mercy"—at which point you might wonder where it is you are standing, in reality or myth, and what is happening to you? Nothing is happening, one poem suggests, in its irony perhaps, but then these are the times when ironies have long become facts since—

blood wasn't spilled
(thank gods for that)

books weren't ripped apart
(thank gods for that)

houses weren't set on fire
(thank gods for that)

bodies weren't riddled with bullets
(thank gods for that)

limbs weren't cut off with knives
(thank gods for that)

only the spirit flew high
(higher, higher, higher)

So, is it irony, dear reader—might I ask—or is it perhaps a se-
ries of subtitles for a documentary of our days. Your call. As
for Nina Kossman, her camera keeps moving its lens across
the landscape that's time—taking us from ancient days to our
own, with a detour that lets us stop by to wave hello at Circe,
Achilles, Theseus and the nymphs, yes, but also at the heroes
of French Revolution. And Pied Piper is there too, and a few
characters from a Russian fairy tale, and Jonah with his whale,
and Giordano Bruno. Among this generous echoing across
halls of time, there is also personal pain: the poet speaks about
her veteran father's silences about war. And the poet's mother,
too, is not far behind. "At last, I found a city," the speaker of
the poem says:

in which my mother still lives.
Old, but alive,
old, but walking

When the mythological and personal meet, something transforms for this reader, perhaps that very "semblance of meaning in a meaningless world" comes to the surface. What is that meaning, you might ask. Perhaps it is awareness of how one isn't alone, after all, and has never been alone on this planet, despite what humanity's so-called "progress" seems so intent to insist on:

> See how they watch you:
> a neighbor's dog
> lying supine at your feet,
> cats in every alley
> with a hungry look,
> a young woman on the ground,
> with a baby in her arms,
> they all watch you.

Words too, watch us. This poet comes to understand this: "Words, you lay in my hand like pebbles, / round and peaceful." But then something happened. What? "But sounds of war came from far away." Yes. And that is the moment when myth can't quite transform history. History pushes through, with its document of a bloodied finger poking us in the eye. And the poet sees that, too:

> A bomb said to a city:
> "I'm falling."
>
> The city asked:
> "Whose side are you on?"

And the bomb responded. What did the bomb respond with,

you might ask. But you already know dear reader, don't you? The bomb kept falling. The poet Nina Kossman wrote these words before she went to war zones in Ukraine. The book is in front of you. Open it, and try to make sense of history and its myths, yes. Or, don't. Perhaps it is enough to dwell with the words—the silences between lines give us hospice. In times like these, that's no small thing; such lyric moments are perhaps not unlike full breaths of fresh air a solitary traveler between historical moment and myth can still take, as they stop to rest a bit between here and their destination, which is, alas, God's unfinished business.

Ilya Kaminsky

I

Ismul the Boy Warrior

(A faux re-creation of an ancient Akkadian text)

If you pity him whose throat you have to cut,
you will not do it. Pity is the enemy of action.
He who acts must rip pity out of his soul,
and stamp on it fiercely with both feet,
with both feet he must take life out of pity.
Because that is the way to take life out of man.
If you are ready to fight like a man in an open field,
you must trample with both feet on your wriggling pity.

Ridicule him who does not step on his pity,
but be on the lookout for him too,
for he may change without you noticing it
and then make mincemeat out of you.
If you want to be a warrior who always wins,
you must stamp out your pity before it stamps out you.
For he who dares not kill his pity,
will not be a warrior who pleases his king.
He will be left alone in the open field,
a feast for a god of worms he will be,
supper for a god of vultures he will be,
tears for his mother, absence for his wife.

Anyone who heard of warriors, had heard of Ismul.
No warrior on earth was better than Ismul.
He defeated heroes from far and near.
He drove out the armies of Emih and Nagur.
Ismul was the best of them all because he had stamped out his pity.
There was a time when even he had a big load of pity. He cried
when they brought Shimus his father back from the field
where Nagur's soldiers did what they had to do.

When they brought home his father's body,
and the boy Ismul saw what had been done,
the boy ripped pity out of his own body
like a weak muscle of no use,
for he wanted to be of use to Shimus his father
who no longer would see Ismul as before,
from the near, but only from a distance
of a spirit that looks on from above.

Woe to him who does not avenge his father,
woe to him who forgets his mother's tears:
soon enough he will find that they flow for him.

Shimus' spirit guided the boy Ismul when
he went from house to house, gathering
young men, sons of those who, like Shimus,
were brought back from the field lifeless
or not brought home at all. His father's spirit
rode with the boy when he rode in front of his army,
as the spirits of other boys' fathers rode with them;
his father's spirit let him know the time to attack.

But when the battle began and the blood was pouring,
the spirit of Shimus left his son's side
for spirits do not like the sight of big blood
and flee the clanging of metal.

When Shimus' spirit flew high into the sky,
it saw the spirits of enemy fathers, a whole army of them,
and there were more of them, and they were stronger
than his son's army. The enemy army had sturdier
swords, swifter horses, and they had big shields

made of pure gold, each like a deadly sun.
Shimus' spirit flew higher, and higher still,
for he wanted to have a word with the gods,
but the spirit could not find the gods anywhere,
not in the upper world, not in the place where they are not,
for where we do not see them is where the gods abide.

"Tell me the outcome of the battle, ye gods,
green, and purple, and bluish-black gods,
gods shaped as animals, and gods shaped as fishes,
bird-gods, frog-gods, and gods shaped as men!"
But in reply all he heard was silence.
The terrible silence of the empty sky.
For the gods had hidden; the gods had fled.
This was not a war they approved of.

Then a single thin cloud came nearer,
and Shimus' spirit was flying inside it,
the spirit was merged with the cloud,
the cloud which was none other than Otz,
the god of unfinished business.
This is what Otz said to Shimus' spirit:
"I praise you for helping your son,
for the boy must avenge your murder.
But this war is to have no winners.
None shall prevail in this battle,
for we gods have had enough warm blood
and are no longer thirsty. Living worshippers
are more pleasing to us than blood.
Fly back to your son's army, spirit,
and whisper into your son's ear
'The gods order you to make peace.' Meanwhile,

I shall order the spirits of the enemy army
to turn their sons away from the battle
with neither defeat nor victory,
but only obedience and humility
to serve and worship the wisdom of the all-seeing gods."

Shimus' spirit could not say anything,
for how can a mere spirit respond to a god?
But when the cloud receded, he saw another.
The other cloud was another god,
all-powerful Iannon it was, god of death
and of completed vows, and this is what
Shimus' spirit heard: "You must not keep your son away
from this righteous battle, spirit.
Do not heed the god of unfinished deeds.
For all that is done is done for the highest,
the god of all gods, in the scheme of schemes."
Then that cloud, too, receded
and Shimus' spirit encountered no more gods
on its flight through the twilight heavens.

The spirit flew through the sky, and flew
until it was near Ismul's army,
and it hovered over Ismul's head,
not knowing what to tell him, which god's advice was correct.
As it looked around it and saw the sky
in whose middle it flew, every cloud
seemed to sprout a god-like shape.
So torn was the spirit between the gods' orders,
that it hovered above Ismul like a quivering fog.
And because it hesitated so,
and because it was at a loss for what to advise,

for which god's injunction to give to Ismul,
Ismul grew suddenly weak as though by witchcraft,
his own spirit went out of him,
and he no longer knew what he was.

Ismul, the bravest boy-warrior, the boldest,
who out of his own soul had built a shield,
no longer could brandish his only weapon,
the blood-drenched sword he had forged himself
from two metals: revenge and courage.
Because his father's spirit was torn in two,
Ismul fell on the ground as though stricken,
as though pierced by an enemy sword.
And even though Ismul was of superior strength,
he was nothing but an empty vessel now, a thing,
a piece of defeated flesh. That is what happens
when a father's spirit is torn between
the commands of cloud-shaped gods.

Seeing that Ismul had fallen, Ismul's army of
ragged boys fled too, and they fled so fast
that the spirits of their fathers could not keep up.
And the enemy warriors, with their sunlike shields
now dull yellow, spiritless yellow like bile,
they too fled at the sight of the fallen Ismul,
instead of rejoicing and furthering their gains:
for they knew that the gods were near.
When the gods are near and at war with each other,
everyone knows it is no time for mortals to fight.
For a man who is caught in the gods' quarrel
is defeated forever, in this life and in all
his lives to come he is condemned to relive his defeat.

That is why Ismul was left alone in the field,
abandoned by all—enemies, friends, and his father's spirit—

Alone in the field with the dead and the dying;
and even his soul left him, although he was not dead.
There Ismul's body lay, without its soul:
the soul left the body and flew.
His soul flew high and low, without direction,
like a butterfly that had lost its way.
Higher and higher rose the wind;
and the stronger it blew on the soul,
the higher and wider the soul flew.
Ismul's poor, bewildered soul, flapping invisible wings,
frightened and lost, completely
alone in the empty sky.
But the emptiness was gradually turning solid;
Little by little it was becoming as dense as
Ismul's own remembered flesh.
Only this was not flesh; this was firm ground;
as solid as anything the soul had seen
in its life on earth within Ismul's body.
More solid than flesh, yet lighter than air,
and visible only to souls' eyes.
It was the city of souls. Where souls were gods.
Here souls slept, played, grew sick, and recovered,
before returning to earthly bodies
and to bodily pleasures and tasks.

What Ismul's soul learned in the city of souls is never revealed:
a lesson equal to no lesson it could have learned in the flesh.
When it was his soul's time to return to his mortal body,

....

of all the precious gifts proffered to it by the souls
it took only one: a transparent jar of pity.
Liquid pity sparkled in the jar like a superior wine.

....

When Ismul's soul flew close to Ismul's body,
it poured pity over his limbs and chest,
and it opened Ismul's mouth and poured the rest down his throat.

And only when Ismul's body was drenched in pity,
was Ismul's soul ready to re-enter the young man's flesh.
Then Ismul arose from the field of battle
and went off by himself, only gods know where.
His army of ragged young men came to him
from every corner of the Amkabadian land.
And when they were gone, rumors were heard of them,
they were said to be seen here and there,
without their swords and shields, yet untouched
by an enemy weapon. Heroes! Heroes of a different sort!
And where they passed, the land became fertile.
Soon all of Amkabadia was in bloom,
for they walked it for years in the steps of Ismul,
their leader whom they called the Conqueror—
not of men but of his own heart.

Valley of Closed Eyes

1

In this second decade of the third millennium
I,
born three times of the tree of flesh,
fallen thrice from its empty branches,
the diaphanous heap of water,
red from the maternal sea,
syllables of my name rushing to rescue
your lips
stillness
air
your lips are trying to form as my name—
complaints of the wind over the heap
of bones.
This be my name in this life:
The Sky Rushing to Meet the Water.

2

Stony water
colored by wind,
chiseled by the light fallen off your eyelids:
one moment is all in the silence of the newborn.
Now take a pitcher,
pour out small echoes, equally
onto the earth,
onto the scorpio fortress,
upon the transparent stones,
and the motionless flame at the door.

3

Dipping my cheekbones
into the blind substance,
into the cooling water of the maternal sea,
I, river of your body,
I, the tightrope of fear your body walks,
return to you nightly, motionless,
daily, nightly
I bury both hands in your solitude:
echoes
answer me in your valley of closed eyes.

4

Salt of the earth in a sunflower seed,
salt on the leaves of the tree of destruction,
salt opening and closing
like a flower,
transparent
labyrinth I must pass
to close my eyelids with your fingers of sleep
to open yours with my fingers of clay and water.

5

In the second decade of the third millennium,
I,
hallucination of flame on the face of a child,
the guardian of the child's aerial dreams,
all of his breaths now a single breath,
all of his words an unending sentence,

I split myself into parallel moons,
I spill myself into a bowl of blood—
You will see me the salt of your body,
you will hear me think in your thoughts...
When I offer to you one face of the moon, you know:
my face is the face eaten away
by years of sickness and hunger,
face of a child who died
fifty years ago.

Shadow over the Town

Helen's shadow on the Trojan rocks
still threatens the Greeks,
burdens them with the highest taxes
the loved exacts from the lover:
middle-class teashop warmth forsaken,
adding machines count the killed,
a scarce spring, a fruitless autumn,
quiet markets and barren cribs:
see the wretched pass for the mad,
the mad for the licentious
shadows creeping after the main
shadow over the town:
the feared outlines of the woman
washed clean of mercy,
memory of the guilt reflecting
future centuries' blood.

Nothing Happened

blood wasn't spilled
(thank gods for that)

books weren't ripped apart
(thank gods for that)

houses weren't set on fire
(thank gods for that)

bodies weren't riddled with bullets
(thank gods for that)

limbs weren't cut off with knives
(thank gods for that)

only the spirit flew high
(higher, higher, higher)

and fell down to earth
(down, down, down)

and no, it wasn't trampled on
(thank gods for that)

the silly spirit should have remembered the rules
(really, it should have remembered them)

flying is forbidden by the gods
(thank gods for that)

Leda

To recall the fear that had overwhelmed her soul,
something had seized her throat so she couldn't cry
out to them, white birds, wild, light, drifting
in the sky which had turned the most remote black.
White birds in black sky, white scream in her throat,
hair splashing the shoulders chased by the awesome bird

hung in lulled air like an ancestor's soul, heavy,
languid, and waiting for an infusion of flesh—
another fill of forgetfulness, heaving,
not hiding her—like a mirror refusing a look
at herself from behind her startled shoulder;
the familiar landscape fleeing from her cry for help,

perhaps at the behest of a god, with his sad mortality,
knowing the images to be thus seized and begotten
from this shivering flesh—wild birds, flying,
no, words, healing...white and fleeting, up in the lightened sky.

To recall that alone, she of all women, she,
the mother of the nation of mythmakers, the generation of
myth transforming itself into memory—man
or god, taking her moistened lips; his voice,
chasing her, has become her children's; light,
gentler than her memory still not in her full command,

lighter, with gentler movements, more tact, less mythology,
the singing without the myth within; in the
time allotted for myth-making—her children singing
in the space allotted for healing music; sounds
that she remembered to have been the ones...
One last time they seized her throat: wild, black birds, fly...

Daphne Speaks

I will grow myself quiet leaves
in the difficult silence of chastity.

I will hide in the immense namelessness
though each tree murmurs to him my name.

I am the bed of leaves he can never scorch,
not even with his eyes of fire.

I am the naked face of the flower; a cross.
He cannot escape by reaching me.

The god and the goal; the lover and the loved;
the pursuit and the flight, entwined.

Though a god, he will die in the depths of my bark.
I will glisten his face on my leaves.

Every eagle will have his eyelids.
Every event—his speed.

Each one of the thousand suns
will pursue me as he has chased.

Each one of the symbols of silence
will learn his name I refuse to bear.

I am he: the sun, its immense bowl
pouring out selves as from a fount of chastity.

He is I: the ever-green song in flight,
the sun forever pursuing me.

Hades' Love

Naked leaves sifted nightly,
gathered, fondled, and stored
in long sheets of black fire,
free of feelings' clatter,
freed most of all from the earth
whose fingertips touched fire, arms
steeped in the sickness of its craving:
Hades' love is persistence; rust;
time spread over wide pastures; weeds
perpetuate the difficult love:
earth over leaf, thuds of jealousy,
black, over the shapeless earth.

Alcestis

Dread husband's mirth
and his new meek tenderness
as even his barest wish,
shaken out of midnight moon,
seeps white love-riddles
into your clasped bones.
Pile, raise dawn-stones
upon your night pain;
consumed in bird echoes,
sigh; dare steal the air
he loves like a rapt beast;
cling to his loveless tenderness
with leaps of a bird's shade
without the shape to sway him
in your shadow's skin.

Words for Danton

If you hadn't learned how to write the word "execution"
before you learned how to write the word "pardon,"
my friend Danton,
you should have become a watchman,
not a revolutionary;
and if you enter a sanctuary like a beggar
with a severed head,
God is your judge,
my friend Danton.
That is why he is a god, you know,
so as not to give alms to every man entering
without a head on his neck.
Fear not, my friend Danton,
that is why you are a revolutionary.
And to rid your heart and your hand of fear,
temper your soul, learn to write the word "execution,"
and right after it, the word "block,"
my friend Danton.
You are neither a boy,
nor a coward,
my friend Danton,
you know how to swim in blood
like in the sea.
You, who drowned in it.

Three Poems about a Head

1

And you, who came here wearing rings,
but without your head,
leave your rings by the door,
and put your head on:
heads are hanging on hooks like hats.
It is unbecoming to enter my house without a hat.
Whichever head you take off the hook,
that head will be yours:
if you take a murderer's head.
you will become a murderer;
if you take a fool's head,
you will become a fool.
But if you're lucky enough to get a wise man's head,
you'll live your whole life as a wise man.
You get what you deserve, as they say.
You get what you—
for not being able to tell the difference between a good head
and a bad one,
for not knowing, not understanding, not being able to.
And if you start whining on your way to your execution,
"All heads on hooks look the same,
the head of a wise man,
the head of a fool,
the head of a murderer..."
Whine all you want—
you are the bearer of your head, not me,
you are its owner and its master,
and you will be held accountable, not I.
And, you know, it is not you who will be led to a scaffold,
no, not you, fool with someone else's head of a murderer,

but the lucky man with that wise man's head:
isn't it foolish to choose a head in a dressing-room like a hat,
without bothering to see what's inside it?

2

If you come to the palace with a sword,
the door is closed to you.
If you come without a sword, but with a key,
you are welcome, my friend Brutus.
If you cut off your left hand and leave it lying on the ground,
it will grow miraculous berries
to cure everything,
except the inability to think.
If you cut off your right hand and bury it in the garden,
it will grow into a little daughter with wings instead of arms.
And if you take my brain on a tray to the forest,
it will grow into Vasilisa the Wise,*
so wise,
that you, with all of your famous wisdom, will be just a chip
    on her shoulder.
And do you know that Vasilisa has a silk handkerchief,
which makes thousands like you keep mum?
And you, too, keep mum, yes, you, too!
If you cut off your leg and serve it to the king for dinner,
what will you get?
You'll be praised,
promoted to a higher rank,
maybe even promoted to valet,
without being asked

――――――――――

* Vasilisa the Wise — a character in Russian fairy tales

whether or not you want the promotion.
So it is much better, my friend, that you do not cut off
your foot or your hand,
and live as you are, whole,
or who knows where your self-sacrifice will take you
and on whose dinner plate your neck will end up.

3

If you lost your head from love for your son,
look for it everywhere,
pull it to you by its hair,
put it back on your neck,
glue it back in place with whatever you can find.
Here it is, where it belongs, your head.
You need it more than your son does.
Frankly, he does not need it at all,
just as he does not need you.
Only you need you. Live for yourself!
As for all those thoughts—what a beautiful baby your son was,
and how you carried him in your arms,
and how you taught him to walk,
and how you held his hand,
and how you fed him and held his bottle,
and how you carried him to sleep every night—
forget all that.
Repeat now: I live for myself only.
Let that be your motto,
Repeat it a hundred times.
Yet you keep saying:
"I've lost my head for the love of my son,
I cannot find it anywhere!"

Well, then live without it.
Your son is lost to you and it is not your fault;
yes, lost to you forever.
Repeat: forever.
Repeat it until you're sick to your stomach.
But find that head and stick it back on your neck.
Use nails, glue, spells, powder, whatever works.
(You know, walking around without the head would not be
     the right thing to do.)

His Happiness

The actual event was no longer of any interest.
A destiny, exquisitely thought through, had folded into a life.
So much for the fluctuating approximations
of intelligent power, purposeful sky.
He tested his strength in the essential instances
when the life and the image flap their joined wings.
Earth, to him, was a belligerent sphere
that spewed forth, on occasion, almost perfectly rounded words.
Yet it no longer mattered what he concocted
the night before, what sonnet of leaves or loss.

In the window he shifted his angle of vision
onto a cloud that shifted its angle of flight.
He thought: nothing sad in the death of contemporaries;
they shift their angle of life into their thorough work.
That he, too, was but a shifting reflection,
not as a stone or grass, no, so much less real than they —
this was an island of thought in an ocean of selfsame melancholy.
Disguised as a graceless chrysalis, it proceeded to unfold its wings.
Look at it! —Seize it! — shut it into your cage of ecstasies!
The happiness unforeseen, the most singular secret of all.

Syrinx

The nymph
flees from him who desires her,

the water knows what equals it:
fire—Pan—goat.

O Syrinx, o water-nymph,
your innocence,

your remote, reflective will
sways, green and supple,

on the bank of Pan's forest-brook:
reed,

you're now the soughing of
the wind, in distance

and ether;
the measured pace;

the sound,
(like an echo,

without a body:
Pan's greed for a mirror)

how you weep,
mother to Memory,

mere leaf, turmoil,
the muse's nurse,

your madness turned to
prophetic gift,

piping.

Ariadne

Over and over
the darkness of sands,
the stillness of waves.
a tangled thread
saved Theseus' life.
Ariadne's gift
became Ariadne's fate:
a gift to be abandoned
on a leaf-shaped island.
Solitude is a gift.
Theseus was so generous with gifts.
Thank you, Theseus,
for sailing away when I slept.
I woke up on Naxos alone
I saw your ship sailing away.
No better gift than solitude.
Thank you, Theseus, she said over and over.
I was just a girl, nothing but mortal flesh,
now I'm a constellation in the sky.
A silly thread made me what I am.
Thank you,
over and over
the darkness of sands,
the stillness of waves.

Demeter's Torch

While you wait for the music to open like a flower,
it is waiting for you to open yourself
to the air from which it is made: this air is you,
the best part of you, the part that is music,
so that your air and the air of music
can mingle like angels mingle with the sky,
or like a tiger that becomes one with the jungle,
or like a torch in the hands of a worshipper,
                              one with mystery,
or, like Persephone, becomes one with the gate
through which she must walk to Hades.

Listen: a torch of music, purple like a hyacinth in early spring,
Look: I am tone-deaf, yet I beg for a song
that will carry me from spring to summer,
from summer to early autumn and then to death,
No, not the foam of Aphrodite but Demeter's purple torch,
the mingling of the air and time at the instant
when the daughter and the mother are one,
when the mother becomes the daughter
and the daughter becomes an adult,
and the mother's longing for the daughter,
and the daughter's parting from the mother
makes flowers everywhere bloom and wither, flower and wilt:
It is open now, the gap in the air that will make you one with
      the music.
Do not resist it! Be silent! Carry the purple torch!

Thetis to Achilles

"What is it, she said,
 that strange mask you put on?
It sticks to your face
and you can't pull it off anymore,
no matter how hard you try.

"Not that you ever try to pull it off,"
she mused after a brief silence.
"You're quite happy with this mask
which you like to think is your new self.
But even if you fool the entire world,
did you really think you could fool your mother?
I know you, I'm all too familiar
with that scrawny boy you want to forget.

 Now, with this shield, this helmet,
and this mask of a warrior —
even if everyone believes you're the tough guy,
the warrior, the real man, the hero,
the conqueror of the Trojans,
do not assume that I, too, will be fooled by it.
Do not come to your mother and act
like the hero that you are to the world,
Hector's killer, the Achilles of the myths
reinvented by old Homer.
Love can see underneath any shield or mask,
and if you prefer to believe
you are something that you are not,
why, you are free to do so, but—

I remember holding my boy by his pink heel,
I remember dipping my boy in the waters of the Styx,
I remember making my boy stronger than anyone—

and don't you tell me that I'm just a silly woman,
or that I don't know that you are that boy,
or that your vulnerable heel is the only real place on your
whole body.

No use trying to fool your mother, tough guy.
She knows you better than you know yourself.

Circe to Odysseus

"What was it," she said,
"the shadow that crossed your face,
and that gesture that looked like a farewell wave?
Remember, I am not her,
not Penelope, remember this,
and even though you are Odysseus,
there is no need for gestures on my unhappy island;
here everything is clear without them.
We see into each other's souls without words or waves,
and if you wish to sail further,
you can do so without shadows,
unnecessary rituals, words, or flowers
that grow on a far-away continent
where summer is winter and winter is spring."

Lament for Odysseus

Beauty that you take so lightly,
because it is not yours,
because it is foreign,
because it is not the beauty of Ithaca,
because it belongs to that other land,
Troy,
the enemy,
the vanquished land,
whose soldiers it was your job to kill,
whose mothers lament in a different tongue
(although the tongue is the same,
yes, it is,
really, it's the same tongue as yours!)
and although you so despise
that foreign beauty
of the land
of buildings
of women,
it is still beauty, Odysseus,
and you know it
in the depths of your clever heart.

Odysseus

Which cry of battle or banner,
which torturous empty rock,
which island bereft of titans,
which beauty lost in the sea
call to you this time, wanderer,
the cleverest of all the Greeks,
where are you lost this time,
what land shall give you shelter,
temporary as all shelters have been,
which Ogygia, Aeaea, or Crete
you shall call your transient home,
you, to whom Penelope is still faithful,
needlessly, old and withered king.

Telemachus

Stranger to the seas,
stranger even to the land that the sea surrounds,
humming a monotonous song
in a language he doesn't know,
a language he forgot long ago,
when he played, a child, at Odysseus' feet,
the father who had been wiped off his memory
so completely that only this humming,
without words or meaning, remains.

How Cassandra Became Clairvoyant

So. You are Apollo. Well, that's a new one.
As good a line as any to get a girl.

A godhead must be like a flowering tree,
open in every pore. But you
are closed in upon yourself.

Devious god, I see right through you.
You guard the image that protects the space
in which you hide, aloof and conscious godhead.

Grant you your desire?
But I'm only an image in your dream,
an inverse reflection of yourself,
a bit of instinct, a bit of soil...

Love you?
Foolish god, I'm a mortal girl,
I cannot love a consciousness,
perfection of a mind that is god.
Besides, I'm not a starry-eyed virgin from a story-book,
although I may look like one to you
as I stand here discoursing with an emptiness,
the disembodied space that claims to be a god.

We trade?...
Lord of the lyre, master of song, lord of prophecy,
king of praise and of timely whispers,
prove now that you are you,
and not an empty cloud begging for a shape.

My wish?
To have the future at my fingertips!
To have the power of your priestesses, Apollo,
but without the laurel-chewing nonsense, if you please:
I'd get a headache from all the chewing.
Measure the price of my body in prophecy:
how many foresights am I worth?

Grant you your desire?
Now that I am a goddess as much as you are a god?

Who do you think you are kidding, lover?
The scales of the future are eloquent, delicate, quick.
A kiss, only one, don't ask for more.
I must go. To Troy, to tell them.
I owe you nothing, lord of good manners,
god of frost and diluted dreams.

Back to your void, Apollo.

Cassandra to Agamemnon

I've warned you of a bloodbath:
a bath, with your blood in it, literally.
But there you go, blundering right in,
no hand of fate can stop you,
the hand that wants you dead.
And I, who will be killed soon after you,
why should I care—when, or of whose hand.
So don't stall—go on, go in,
step blindly into your matron's trap,
hero of the great war, great murderer yourself.
Before I die, I'll see you flounder,
like a fat carp, in the fishnet of your queen.
But what is this water in my eyes?
My eyes that have seen my brothers killed,
My city razed, before and after.
Nobody weeps for you, therefore I will.
I, Cassandra.

Agamemnon's Shadow Speaks

Too many thoughts
mind too small
crowded there
inside

he said

Give me more brain
make me a genius
or else

I'll steal your cow
I'll make war
I'll kill your men
you kill mine

said Agamemnon
or one of the other pot-bellied kings

too many men
too little bread
what to do
let's make war

said he of the big belly
and of the big mustache
chief of the walled city
Mycenae
maybe no worse than Troy

our women you know
they don't run around
from city to city
like what's her name
because of whom this war

they stay put
inside the walled city
they don't betray you with a stranger
better with the next of kin

when they kill you
it's straightforward
in a bathtub
with a fishnet
you come home from work—and bam!
no time to regret

no big war
no Troy
no army

it's between you and your spouse
and maybe your concubine
Cassandra
why was she underfoot
she with her prophecies
so she goes too

not too much blood
very orderly

then your spouse rules
with her new spouse
he next of kin
we are all blood relatives here

call my slaves
wash off my blood
until my bathtub is sparkling clean

I told this story too many times
feeling tired now

said Agamemnon's shadow

Gods out of Rock

"I made picture upon picture in my mind,
I made picture upon picture of my gods,"
said Lydia, who was known for wanting to live forever.

"For my love of them,
I built gods out of rock,
out of wood,
out of clay,
out of words,
out of metal,
all of them broke,
all them crumpled,
decayed,
turned into dust.

Until one day
I started making different gods,
or rather, goddesses,
all in the image of my own self,
yes, my own little self,
and these images stayed,
they are the only ones that last,"
said Lydia, who was known for wanting to live forever.

"And I shall continue carving them
out of marble,
wood,
metal,
and words.
Let people think I make them
simply because I love myself so much
—Let them—

I know better.
If someone asks,
"Why do you make image upon image of yourself, Lydia?"
"I simply want to make things that last," I shall say.
Even when I make an owl from marble,
it is myself,
and it shall last."

Thus spoke the living goddess,
who herself did not last very long.

In the City of Delphi

In the city of Delphi,
where bloody games
take the place of prophecies
and of peaceful games,
shadows of priests and Pythias,*
and of those who, for prophecies,
paid only what they could—
a slave, a rooster, a horse, a coin;

in the city of Delphi
life is like an old net,
only tourists and guides get caught in it.
And I, too, am caught in this tattered net.
I can't untangle it,
can't figure out where am I,
where is the Pythia,
where's the priest,
where's the rooster,
where's the horse,
where's the coin,
and whose voice is whispering to me:
— Stay,
you yourself are the Pythia.
As for the coin and the horse,
forget them.

---

* *Pythia (or Oracle of Delphi) — priestess dedicated to Apollo*

All Alike

The bitter loss
of a wood nymph
fleeing from the winner,
entangled in the underbrush,
the laurel, the grass, the reeds...
Alas, gods are all alike:
it takes courage to flee from them
into the darkness of myth;
and the ones who succeed in fleeing,
just as those who stay,
are but innocent trophies—
not of the lecherous gods,
but of mythmakers
who brought them to life.

Wolves

See, they are back,
with an awkward trot, from the hills.
No, not horses; no spurs clanging,
no curved moon on their brows,
even though stars roll under their feet,
like they rolled for their ancestor, the golden sun.
Higher! Halloo! Hold it!
Whisperings of snow frightened off by the hounds,
splintering twigs of air.
There they are! The wolves!
The ones who terrify the moon!
Now they are pursued by my voice, thin yet hoarse.
And the goddess of air herself
Hides them in her womb.
See: no, not the blue snow—it is the darkness,
its tender arms unwoven,
the kind darkness

II

Untitled 1

A little reason carries us a little way.
The hero dies before the narrator
comes to a final stop. Applause!
The rider seeks his steed, the moralist—
his Book. The audience claps for HIM,
HIM again: "Those heroic shoulders, that earnest smile!
He is alive! He is back! He is resurrected!"
The squirming face takes over the scheming gesture.
Wrapped in expensive rags, the painted lovers
rewrite a prologue to that eventual disaster,
their love. The hero is one of them, or one
of them is he. His eyes the color of his strength;
his solitude, bitter. Applause is but the assurance
of a more total end, he murmurs as the audience claps.
He juggled life and death, taking part in neither.
His solitude is unrelieved; his reason, gone.

Imagine Two

I have too clear a mind for dreaming,
she said as she ordered her thoughts away
from the distances they were meant to approach
and surround with incantations of thought,
with benedictions that carried cloudiness
into the world of too much logic and fact—
to make the most prodigiously dancing statement,
to make the most motionless music speak.

As she said what she said, newer thoughts
formed a tangible world of their own—
with the sky, and the grass, and the earth
furiously alive, furiously real, peopled
as if by mistake, by the same unidentified men
who demanded their newly made lives be a story
—differences seen, advantage of each admitted—
and that she be the one to tell:

"In the definition of oneself, what is oneself
but what the mind of another has one be?
A stage of flux, a cycle of expression,
a monad of breath, half-fish, half-bird,
a human fully conscious of oneself,
a story of a life not fully told yet imagined
with all the colors one can see and sense
in all four worlds susceptible to love and color?"

She would be fair: she would define each
through his honest love of her, that being
an amorphous and hard-to-define thing
not lending itself easily to scales or rulers,
laurels of glory or medals of perfection,

well-sharpened wits or post-scientific methods
of finding the culprit by the manner of his deeds,
the manner of his thoughts remaining doubly hidden.

She would be fair; she would collect from each
a love of just his size and shape of mind,
no more than his imagination could contain and give—
a well-formed thought, an inchoate cry, a foppish praise
not so much beautiful or kind but truthfully
the shadow enshrouding his uninvented self
which loved because it lived: not she—
the object of his love but he—love's origin and meaning.

She would give back to each one his identity. Each
would have a story so suited to his needs
that every word would strike a memory
in his not so newly hatched as newly defined love
mimicked with new meanings yet as century-old
as himself. A story of his love would be her definition
of what he was and what he would become,
when all chimeras of his own making

fly to the other side of consciousness,
while the reality of clouds, snow, rain
is brusquely shoved away from heaven,
then poured into his lap as well imagined
as only true things can be. Alive and moving,
always turning back into himself,
his mask of words glistening with newer definitions,
he is himself at last. And he is hers.
One of the many becomes the only one whose story
grows to be punctuated by exclamations of her love

of long ago, well before she made him up:
her thought, an artifice in the artificial world,
created him, a man, in the world of rain and snow,
a man in the world of things that breathe and wonder
at man's being one with trees, her as a tree
whose branches sway to give him shade, repose.

Life Within a Museum

To see the faces of men, remote and deep,
remote, as in a listener singing without words,
singing and seeing the processions of thousands
waiting for the picture to drift and sing
organize into prismatic perceptions
the unkempt indifference of their wish.

To see the wish grow ripe in the images darkly golden,
darkly painted as the whole stands darkly seen;
desire golden the aura of centuries painted real,
recollected within the shadowy clearness of a mind within
a sea of images, a sea of birds, a birth within
a sea, foam like wings, new birth, new air.

To see the images unravel life within life,
fertile and thickening at the edges—a defense
against life's awkward movements to dislodge
its seed; to turn it limp, and damp, and swarming
with images of the past again—a star, an axe,
salt on the axe and in the throat.

Music will be salty, too: overwhelmed
with images like sounds, shadows dissolving into song,
shadows conversing in unreal tongues, unreal echoes,
air drifting words in voiceless paraphrases, painted men
under a painted star, fishing for the future nestled in the sea
like in a womb, the safest citadel of singing

birds flapping wings imagining alarm:
"The womb has lost its power to create!"
without voice, without words, these golden faces
sing of the past—the salt, the axe,

the air drifting in while they stand frozen—
the guards, the public: a museum still.

Untitled 2

The child was inside me,
and when she emerged,
Creation was singing around us.
The child grew big and left,
and when she returned,
she could not see me
and could not hear me,
and Creation that had sung around us,
was mute.

Untitled 3

My mind used to move
    like a swift lizard,
      from stone to stone.
And now it hangs
    like an empty cocoon
      that will never become a butterfly.

Untitled 4

You are a force
deep inside me
that doesn't know my name.
(See me throw it into the fire.)

That, deaf to my entreaties,
wouldn't rescue me
from a burning house.
(See me throw it into the sea.)

That wouldn't save me
if I were drowning.
And if I drowned, it would drown too.
(See me throw it into a forest.)

That wouldn't look for me
if I were lost in a forest.
(If I were lost, it would be lost with me.)

See me throw it back into me:
How you dissolve, how you melt away,
no longer a force,
just a dead man's soul.

About the Pied Piper and His Flute

Have a drink, he says, so you catch
—no, not a buzz, he says, but a wave.
Aren't people like radios, he says,
radios catch waves,
and so can we.
Not everyone can, of course,
but you could.
Yes, I could, before,
I knew how to do it,
but now I can't
I've lived too long.
I've been far too sober,
I see reality
as it is, not as I want it to be.
It's better this way, I tell myself,
to live in the real world,
without drug-induced visions,
without poetry, without music, without beauty;
it's better this way—
to stand with your both feet on the ground,
firmly and boringly,
to plant your feet on the ground,
and to see reality
the way it really is
instead of jumping on clouds,
from cloud to cloud
like a bird,
like a butterfly, like a moth,
so as to end up on the ground,
always to fall on the ground at the end.

And sometimes a whole nation
sometimes, even an entire country,
millions and millions of people
who were used to believing in beautiful fairy tales,
to read beautiful poems
—only the ones that rhyme!—
poems that mesmerize the readers with their music,
their beauty,
and put a spell on him so he falls asleep, and sleeps, sleeps, sleeps.
It is good to dream to the music of such poems,
and to dream beautiful dreams,
and sleep, sleep, sleep, sleep.

To the accompaniment of such music
even death won't seem too terrible,
and the end will lure you with music,
with pictures, with colors, with sleep...
And when the people, who have absorbed these sounds,
when the people become the sounds,
like a musician becomes a flute;
when such a people finally falls from a cloud,
suddenly falls from the clouds onto the earth,
they don't know what happened to them,
—what happened to you? Are you hurt?
—No, there is no pain now,
pain is what you feel at first and the people are already dead,
the beautiful sounds have drowned out everything in them,
even the pain of the fall,
even the horror of passing,
the fear of extinction
of an entire race -
not just the individual self.

Do you remember the children of Hamelin?
Mesmerized by the sound of the flute,
how they ran after...
"Wait," he says.
The Pied Piper was no ordinary musician,
he played like a god!
That's just it—"he played like a god!"
The sound of the flute, however magical,
was enough
to hypnotize all those children,
to take them to a place from which they had been awaited for
    centuries
and from whence they will never come back.
But do not pity the children: they have not experienced the
    fear of death
and, as they were dying, they had no idea that they had been
    deceived by the Pied Piper,
the Ratcatcher, in other words.

People are not rats, you'd say,
and the legend of the Pied Piper has nothing to do with it.

But, I say, will you get down after all,
you, mesmerized by the sound of beautiful poetry
(I know, I know, you can spend your life in the clouds,
swallowing rhymes, metaphors, etc., etc.),
just try to live without hypnosis,
without rhymes,
without music,
without pictures,
without succumbing to the temptation of surrendering to appeals
("we are a great nation of high culture, etc., etc.").

The landing will hurt,
but only at first,
and when the pain passes
boredom and disgust will set in,
and you will see that while you were up there, flying,
on the ground—they've been killing
in your name!
You will say—no, no, I was flying!
I was high up, I did not know!
The real world is
bloody, ridiculous, unbearable,
and it's impossible to live without anesthesia, hypnosis, some
    kind of a lie.

But still, try to live only in the real world.

And if you go after yet another Pied Piper,
be honest with yourself and say:
I can't live without a hangover lie,
Falling into it again,
even though it feels like flying.

The Tale of Tzarina Alyonushka and Her Brother Ivanushka

(a free-verse version of a well-known Russian fairy tale)

"I warned my brother not to drink from the lake.
I warned him.
But, at that age, do they listen?
He drank from it.
And of course his quick arms and legs
became goat limbs,
his blond curls became white fleece.
—Ivanushka!
Beware, kid brother,
of the witch
and her knives,
her pots full of water.
Her greed fills them up.
Her jealousy heats them.
She is the Queen now.
She wears my face.
She stole my figure,
and I—
I worked so hard at it!
But who can hear my protests?
My voice hardly reaches you
from these stinky depths.
What does she want with us?
Ah, my husband, the Tzar.
Does she hold his hands as I used to?
And when he admires her face
(my cheeks,
my skin,
my mouth)
does he know those eyes

—glass eyes,
or maybe marble, or even granite—
those eyes aren't what they were.
(For a witch can put on another's body,
but never the eyes.)
You're crying, kid brother.
If I could, I'd swim out to you
from this slimy sea bottom,
these weeds that entangle me,
these crabs that bite,
and these fishes that make cruel fun of me.
But the stone on me
is like a planet
thrown off its course
and put to an evil use by her magic.
And all I can do now
is think out these words to you.
Brother Ivanushka!
You're crying again.
Her deadly pots are close to boiling.
Though this isn't a good time for chiding,
let me say to you this:
here's what we've come to,
all of this grief,
and—why?
Only because
when I said: "Do not drink from this lake, brother,"
you threw to the winds my big-sister words of advice.
And so you turned into a baby goat.
But do I blame you?
I don't blame you.
It is her I blame.

You were only a silly child.
Who could tell
this is how you and I would end up?
The sky is so far from the sea-bottom.
Are you still calling out to me?
Ivanushka?"
Here the Tzarina paused.
She didn't like to dwell on misfortune.
So she took a deep breath
and hastened to the end of her story.
"I prayed for the miracle.
Suddenly—
the stone became light,
the weeds loosened from my ankles,
from my knees,
and my elbows;
and up I swam,
up from the slimy sea bottom.
On the shore
Ivanushka ran to me.
His fleece shone like pure gold, sheer happiness.
When my husband the Tzar heard us out,
he had the witch boiled in the same big pot
she'd prepared for cooking Ivanushka.
Though Ivanushka's still a goat,
he's well and alive. We talk.
This is how my miracle happened.
Now, ladies, gentle Tzarinas, tell me about yours."

Purple Men with Houses in the Suburbs Will Never Bother Me Again

Strange little men with purple hands came to me at dawn.
"Your time is up," they said. "You're useless now."
"And who are you?" I asked. "We're messengers of death," they said.
"That's a relief. And now, will you go away, please?"
In response, they stretched their little arms to me
and moved in dream-like fashion, growing now larger, now smaller.
I could see right through them. I could hear them think.
"What does she think she is?" they thought,
as their purple fingers pulled at my liver and my lungs.
"My thoughts are still my own," I groaned, "even if my body is not."
I tried to brush their purple fingers off me,
yet they persisted with that nonsense they called "death."
This gathering of purple creatures can't be real, I thought.
And at this point one of them said,
"I'm real enough—I have a house in the suburbs!"
"No," I said, "this means the distance between us is so great,
You can't do anything to me at all. And now—scram!"
As soon as I said "Scram," the creatures vanished.
Purple men with houses in the suburbs will never bother me again.
Scram! Scram! Scram! Scram!

My Room Has Digested Me

Like Jonah in the stomach of a giant fish,
I sit in the stomach of my room.
Here I sit, day in, day out,
and wherever I turn,
I see junk:
I turn to the left—junk.
I turn to the right—more junk.
My room has digested me and spat me out,
it has taken everything out of me,
like we take everything out of a cow,
its flesh—our succulent dinner,
its skin—our boots,
its stomach enzymes—our oh so yummy Parmesan cheese.
I don't complain.
This is justice.
Let the room digest me as much as it wants.
It's time all of us were spat out
by this once-upon-a time lush and livable planet
as fair payment for turning it into junk.

Conversation with the Earth

I asked the Earth:
"Are you ready?"
and the Earth thought
I was asking if it was ready to die.
So I hurriedly said, "Sorry,
that's not what I meant at all."
I simply asked,
"Are you ready?"
And the Earth replied,
"I'm ready, but it is not I
—no, no, not I—
who is going to die
but you—you—you.
I will be merely transformed
and no longer fit to live on,
and all the creatures that live
on me—and off of me—will perish,
including you—you—you."
Then the Earth asked me:
"Are you ready?"
And I said, "No, I'm not ready to die."
And the Earth said,
"You should hurry, it's time,"
and I said, "Forgive us,
for we know not what we do to you."
And the Earth whispered,
"Goodbye."

Giordano Bruno's Unwritten Letter

It was freezing on the Campo de Fiori on February 17, 1600.
A crowd gathered to watch a heretic burn alive.
There he was, naked, hung upside down,
punished for denying the dogmas of the Catholic Church,
and while the crowd hooted and hollered,
Giordano Bruno, whose mind was still intact,
despite weeks of torture endured by his body,
(the boot* did not suffice to make him recant),
was composing a letter, in his head, to those
who would stand on this piazza centuries later,
when every child would know the obvious facts
for which he was sentenced to burn today:
that the earth revolves around the sun
and not the other way around;
that God is inside us, and not out there,
a bearded man looking on from a cloud,
taking a cue from old men in cassocks;
that freedom of thought was worth striving for,
and even dying for, even torturously burned at the stake.
He didn't have time to complete the letter
which he was composing in his head,
as the flames were beginning to engulf his body,
and even his mind, strong as it was, could not work as before.
"The day will come," he tried to continue in his head,
when everything I wrote would be proven facts…"
This was the last line in Giordano Bruno's unwritten letter.
In a few hours, his ashes would be collected into a bag,
and the bag would be carried to the Tiber. Opened. Emptied.

---

* *"The boot ("the Spanish boot") — a medieval instrument of torture.*

One by One

One by one,
and then another one,
and another one,
we lay down
on the bottom of a pit
your laughter was the last thing we heard,
as you shot a bullet in us.

One by one,
and then by two,
and another two.

Thank you, local collaborators.
Thank you for German bullets.
(Remember the commander's order:
"Bullets are expensive—don't waste them!
One bullet for mother and kid!")

Remember
how you made us dig the pit,
how you made us lie on the bottom,
sardine-style, as your commander
called his brilliant invention.
Digging the pit was hard work.
Lying in it was easy.

We watch you
from the bottom of our pit,
as you succumb to senility
and to all it entails
one by one
and then another one,
and another one,

as you lie
in your gilded coffins,
surrounded by a bevy of grandchildren.
We watch you
as you are lowered into the ground
where we still lie sardine-style,
just like we did on that day
when you machine-gunned us
into this yama.*

One by one by one
our bones come to meet you—
it's an open house day,
we meet-and-greet new guests;
you don't recognize us
but no matter,
we watch you
from the bottom of our pit,
as you lie awake
clumps of earth in your empty eye sockets;
remember
how easy it was,
how much fun you had:
pif-paf, pif-paf!**

One by one,
and then another one,
and another one.

---

* *yama (яма)—Russian for "pit"*

** *Pif-paf! Pif-paf!—onomatopoeia for gunfire, in Russian (similar to
"Bang! Bang!")*

Untitled 5

Time had no claim on him
and beauty had no hold:
in the dried-out backyards of the mind
his soul flowered and observed
the sun setting early in the morning glories,
their petals closing for a day-long sleep,
the dark, arriving full of shadows, concealing
the flowers' future in the opening leaves...
And who was he, to urge them to unfold,
if sleep was what they were meant for in this life,
if their immortality came wrapped in somnolence,
when the air was made of witching words
and sprouted blue and purple petals
that folded into themselves and withered
before he had a chance to see them face to face?

A Statue of Socrates

Apart from
everything that can be marred,
apart from the world,
and apart from peace
(both of which are *mir* in Russian),

apart from beauty
in the eyes of the curious,
together with stars
in the psyche's sky;
here stands a statue
to the one who could fly
better than eagles,
birds of thought
(he said so himself more than once);

here he stands,
freer than all the mortals,
with invisible wings,
beholden to nothing,
except for the words he composed
for himself alone
and for butterflies that circle around his head.

Ash-berries and Acid Leaves

Ash-berries and acid leaves,
burnt acorns and poisoned fruit,
neither poor nor rich
will partake of these berries;
the ill will not become healthy,
while the healthy will become ill.

I have seen the poisoned.
I have seen the ill.
Old symbols did not save them,
Stripped symbols did not save them;
the poor were hungry,
they would eat almost anything,
even the burnt acorn
and poisoned berries and fruit.

Who had the secret thought: nothing will cure us
                            but cure itself?
Who had the secret knowledge: stripping of symbols
                            will not heal the wound?
Who had remembered the words: silence will not cure us,
                            but the anger will do us in?
Who said that symbols belong to history,
which is neither black nor white
but the color of faded pages?
All it can do is teach us
how not to repeat it
again
and
again
and
again.

Symbols Worn Out by Time

What is a flower
that never opens?

What is a word
that remains unsaid?

What is a rock
that does not get thrown?

What is an island
that remains uninhabited?

What is a thought
that remains unfocused?

What is a child
that remains unborn?

What is a homeland
that is forgotten?

What is an animal
that becomes extinct?

What is beauty
that is not set apart?

What are eyes
that do not see beauty?

What is a protest
that does not destroy
symbols that dot the landscape?

What is a landscape
that is made of symbols?

What is history
but new meanings
for symbols worn out by time?

Born Two Days Ago

Fortunate one,
born two days ago,
you have twelve more days to live,
a whole eternity,
depending on how you think about it,
but you don't think
this way or that,
all you do is flap-flap
your pretty wings,
newborn butterfly,
you circle my lilac tree,
it, too, has only one month to bloom;
you don't worry about mortality
nor stay in your room
to guard yourself from the flu,
you're happy
to be alive this moment,
because this moment is life,
and that's all that matters.
Fortunate one,
born two days ago,
you have no memories
of being a helpless cocoon;
why can't we be like you,
beautiful butterfly,
why can't we flap our wings
and be thoughtless
like you.

A Spider and a Rose

An angel who thought he was a spider said:

Hello happy rose.
My love is a spider.
My dog is a mouse.
I hear it bark.

Hello, hello spider.
You and the rose are wind.
Wind, wind. We won.
Whoever heard it bark?

I'll go down the way of a rose.
I'll switch from a song to a blue.
I'll marry a violet.
I'll whine at the moon and cry.

I am a happy flower.
My name is Spider.
I eat whispers.
I drink the best.

I know an angel.
His name is Tom.
Tom-cat, Tom-cat,
God looks at me through your wings.
He wishes to help me whisper.

So many cats.
We angels hide in them.
We are not bats: we are cats.
We are not bad, not good.

We are last.
We sleep in the grass.
We know who you are.
You are a fool.
You are warm.
Your bones are skin.
Your skin has a look.
You look a bully.

—Bully yourself, you!

—We are Angels!

—Angels don't flap their wings at cats.
Angels do not say meow.
Angels... angels... God's angles,
That's what they are!
God folds them angly.

Don't tell me you are an angel.
You are a dog.
Just like I am.
We are like little violets.
We fret and grow.
We like frog concerts.
Sometimes we look green.
Perhaps then, perhaps we are frogs...
We like green snow.
When we go for walks,
Mosquitoes bite us.
That's good,
It shows that we're not them.

Certainty is what makes an angel.
When it rains cats and dogs,

We sleep.

A Score of Fifteen

Here goes a watchful spider
And the sky fades.
In a frolicsome desert
You shall not be dust.
Hee-wee! Hee-wee!
So I say, wish dreams.
In a frolicsome desert,
In the great banal...
How fiery is thy heart, stupor.
How I love thee fade.
Heave steams, you heavers look great
On a finicky face of a faucet.
He who loves the obscure,
Does not love the flesh.
Hee-wee! Hee-wee!
Go spoon me a score of fifteen.
You can spoon me a score of fifteen.
Yes, you can.

I was born here, I lived here...
Now I live in a structure.
Why do I start when I finish?
Hee-wee! Hee-wee!
I am most happy without mice.
Merci. Whatever you say.
Hee-wee! Hee-wee!
You know how to deceive yourselves.

A line, a line:
A river of sudden intellect.
A line, a line...
A brain of exquisite promise.

Ho-ho.
One measure against the speed,
Another—to please you over to my form.
I love the past like a snake—its skin.
Wait, minute.
Add yourself to the hour.
Wait, wait.

Hee-wee! Hee-wee!
Little piggy in the grass:
A river of no promises.

Abstract causes do not benumb me.
I am most fragile when I am two.
Wish dreams: the fish and his funny pose.

Ho-ho!
How fiery is thy wisdom!
Go to the stone, then turn to the right.
When speaking to the stars,
Keep your mouth shut.
I hear little bells,
Softer and softer.
I have lived elsewhere,
I don't remember birth.
Help me, piggy! O my heart's original fervor!
O fish in the pond, o tongues of wings!
Sing to me, sleep's humility.
I so wanted to wish.
But the sky fell ill with emotion,
And I fell into wormy grass.

Birds, let me hear my bones sing.
All birds are air.
All songs sing time.
Time ends when birds flutter.
I don't want them to die!

I'll arch my ankles, I'll dance on my back.
I'll beg Time to give me a hand.
O Time, tick-tock me back into sleep!
Deedle-dee deedle-dee deedle-dee-do.

All stories end.
All flowers melt.
I smell a secret.
And who are YOU?

A Flock

See how a black flock
of silently fallen birds
stares, swallowing air,
at the air, staring down;
and their mind, become wings
and their astonished dreams
of the sky, insidiously sawed
down to its very bluest—
the black flock, without a sound—
into the soundless blades of grass:
an alloy of the hundred-eyed earth
and the seeing sky.

Empty Rock

How far I had to walk
just to be near you,
empty rock,
all that's left of the empire
that once ruled the seas,
not to mention the earth,
the entire world known to men
of the past which is now a shadow
known only to lovers of myth,
as well as to ordinary lovers,
to whom you appear in a dream,
as you twice appeared to me,
empty rock.

Untitled 6

Avoid the lingering memory
of midnight blossom amidst the woods
and don't look at anyone closely:
mortality is contagious.
And when you fall for a human voice,
and it reminds you of godlike emptiness,
remember: what survives is the worst
of human intelligence.

"A semblance of meaning in a meaningless world..."

A semblance of meaning in a meaningless world,
a spire of an old church in the cloudy sky,
ruins of a temple in the desert sand,
a civilization rising from an inchoate thought,
a childhood memory amidst forgetfulness:
this is how I remember a scrawny shrub
on a beach near Mähe, outside of Tallinn,
and my parents spreading a thin blanket for us,
and my brother sitting on it in his plavki,*
and me, on my haunches, next to him,
in my wide underpants, red with white dots,
the kind worn by Soviet girls too young for a bathing suit,
and this is how a semblance of meaning
rises in the middle of a meaningless day—
remembering pebbles on a Baltic beach,
and closer to the water, a city we built from sand,
and a spire of a sand church, to be destroyed
by a foot of a vacationer so intent on a quick dip in the sea,
he gives no thought to what he might step on.
Ruins of a temple on an Estonian beach,
a civilization rising from a child's creation,
a childhood memory, meaning in the midst of meaninglessness,
that proverbial feast which is always with you.

---

* *Plavki (Russian: плавки) — bathing trunks for boys*

See How They Watch You

See how they watch you:
a neighbor's dog
lying supine at your feet,
cats in every alley
with a hungry look,
a young woman on the ground,
with a baby in her arms,
they all watch you,
they all want something from you,
and you think you know very well what it is,
yet when you succumb,
because something in you doesn't let you walk past them,
they ignore your giving hand,
as though to teach you a lesson:
We don't need your paltry offerings, M'am,
because, you see, even beggars have their pride here:
this is the land of the truly free, Sister,
who value something other
than what you can give them.

A Hindu in Kathmandu

He is a holy exception,
the untouchable Hindu.
His soul wanders in purity,
Incarnated as a man.
His soul chisels his bodies;
They are his nameless path.
Even though his fate may flower,
He belongs to it just in half.
Even though he's the bone of energy,
He is also the buried seed.
Even though his blood may be water,
It is not water that satiates.
Even though his tongue is stone,
The tomb he builds will disclose
Lips of silence
Carved on the face of a tree.

A New Love

I have a new love, a new joy,
You can say, it's a new affair:
Not with a man or a woman,
And this time, it's not even a cat.

What a joy to admire
My love's darkly red face!
Although strictly speaking,
It is not a face but a sexual organ,
Male and female combined in one,
Resulting in sheer beauty.

I say to my love:
How can such beauty exist?
It can't. You are an annual.
You will be gone in the fall.
This world is not a place
For a beauty that lasts.

I say to my love:
You and I, like all lovers,
Are aware that we must part.
She listens, mute and serene,
Understanding nothing.

Stay healthy and fill me with joy
Until the end of November,
When your brief life will end
Where it began:
In this brown soil.

Faux Translation from the Akkadian

White upon black,
black upon brown,
blood upon white,
blood upon black,
red upon brown,
red upon black.

All blood is red;
only red.

God's color is unknown
when God is the unknown.

When gods become disposable,
their color becomes known.

When gods are irrelevant,
their skin color becomes relevant.

When a white god is bleeding,
the color of his blood is red.

When a brown god is bleeding,
the color of his blood is red.

Only a bleeding god knows
his worth in the minds of men.

Untitled 8

Wait
till I mold you from clay,
(not you, of course—
only your likeness)
and transplant your soul
into this clay face.
It was your soul
that made you what you were,
not your nose,
your chin,
your cheeks,
your forehead,
but I will mold them anyway,
so your soul feels more familiar
in this unfamiliar place,
since it needs to settle somewhere
after your passing,
and what better place for it
than this clay mold,
although nothing
nothing at all,
you know,
can be as perfect for it
as your own body,
but now that you are dead
and your body is ashes,
this mold is the only home
for your homeless soul.
You know this.

Untitled 9

your thoughts flew like butterflies
over imagined gardens
your thoughts swayed like sunflowers
in rhythm with the wind
your thoughts shined eyes like suns
caught in unpolished copper
caught in the nets of the evening
open-mouthed like fish
your thoughts in their speechless balance
were neither life's songs nor vowels
they burned their hieroglyphic ambers
as clear as unborn suns

Untitled 10

Lines shouldering clipped words,
careful not to wake the sea
of pride in uniform sounds,
impatience brewing in them like wine
in tight-lidded kegs:
an army scattered in emptied ruins
beyond the sky's drifting sight,
versed in swift rising—
now or never. So words defy truce:
carved shafts aiming upward
grammarians can't grasp.

Untitled 11

As I pass your jail door,
I remember you,
free of walls and doors,
locked gates and security guards,
wardens and cellmates,
a "room for visitors,"
and all the accoutrements
of a totally finished life;
I remember you, free,
reading a poem by Yeats,
writing your own poem,
now that your life is over,
and there is nothing I can do
to relieve the pain of memory
but remember you,
free of cell doors and locks,
and of a warden's voice,
saying, "Visiting hours are over, sir."
Over, indeed.
Finally, you are free.

The Wake

In a language unconscious of games,
unconscious of being a language,
a thing apart from yourself,
a silence,
a sea light,
a desire for form,
you speak as the humming darkness,
the breeze,
the sounds of images
envelop your voice.

Let the memory go down
the un-danced road of no-words.
In mid-air, where your childhood home stands,
see the lawn filled with flowers:
the face of a plant or of your mother
no longer living,
yet, all the same, interrupting your life
with her phantom goodness
still visible in your imagination's sleep.

Fiercely,
the child of your own intelligence,
of the forms your intelligence takes in your words,
of the forms that grow golden in the sun
and are grey in moonlight,
of phrases that are spoken once
by shadowy, distant lips,
of meditation too hollow for sleep,
and sleep too light for perfection,

shape your own shadows
from these motionless deaths
in this landscape, motionless
but for the fecund shapes surrounding you,
making indifferent noises
in their unconscious way.

Scatter clusters of syllables,
an apprentice of intelligent void,
solid space acquiring language,
the words that become the void
or settle on your palm like pigeons
cooing their way through your sleep:
memory giving form to memory,
and mastery giving form to pain–
no longer a sound from a misty past,
but a full-blooded flood of sorrow.

Untitled 12

Fruit on a branch
the color of fire,
fruit on a plate
the color of a muted song;
open, fruit,
speak your secret,
before you are eaten,
before you are dead.

Untitled 13

Apple
sun-filled
fruit of a tree of oblivion
so elegant
on your perishable branch
so ripe
in your golden glow
how soon
you fall
to be eaten by worms
or picked
to melt in a child's mouth

Untitled 14

At last, I found a city
in which my mother still lives.
Old, but alive,
old, but walking
all night in my sleep.

What's on Sale Today

First, you sell your time.
(This is called "earning a living.")
Then you sell your ideas.
(This is called "being famous.")
Then you sell your house.
(This is called "moving up.")
Then you sell your wife of twenty-five years.
(This is called "a midlife crisis.")
Then you sell your old books.
(This is called "becoming a real Buddhist.")
Then you sell your old friends.
(This is not called anything special.)
Then you sell your old clothes.
(This is called "crossing the threshold" or simply "poverty.")
Then you sell your conscience.
("But, ma'am, we don't use this word here...")

Woe from It All

"Woe from Wit" is a famous Russian myth.
Woe from thinking too much.
Woe from feeling too deeply.
Woe from not feeling deeply enough.
Woe from saying too much.
Woe from not saying enough.
Woe from not saying anything.
Woe from writing your thoughts.
Woe from writing down others' thoughts.
Woe from not writing anything.
Woe from being different.
Woe from being the same.
Woe from praying to a wrong god.
Woe from praying to the right god.
Woe from not praying at all.
Woe from God.
Woe from man.
Woe from woman.
Woe from a tyrant.
Woe from a crowd that obeys a tyrant.
Woe from a crowd that disobeys a tyrant.
Woe from a pin on your school uniform with the little Ulianov boy.
Woe from not wearing a pin on your uniform with the little
    Ulianov boy.
Woe from thinking too subtly.
Woe from thinking too plainly.
Woe from not thinking at all.
Woe from knowing that the author of "Woe from Wit" was
torn apart by a madding crowd in Tehran.
Woe from it all.*

---

* "Woe from Wit" is a famous verse comedy by Alexander Griboedov, written
in 1823.

"I, who was not killed in any war..."

And I, who was not killed in any war,
who did not march with an army of any motherland,
who did not hide in a trench because I took no sides,
since I had escaped from the motherland's steel clutches
(this motherland or that, makes no difference to me,
the motherland being a figment of the imagination of the crowd,
and the crowd, by definition, is incapable of thinking,
it takes on faith catchwords handed down by its king);
since I have escaped all rulers from an early age, I am free
from the crowd's narrow-browed definition of every word,
I am beholden to slogans neither of the right nor of the left,
both seem tedious to me, like an undercooked oatmeal,
which the mind of the crowd transforms into the best of viands.
I repeat: I was not killed in any war because, like kolobok,*
I escaped from the old woman, the bear, and the wolf,
and there is no one to tell me what to think.
I think for myself: it is no small feat, things being as they are.
I am free to walk in no one's woods, because I belong
to no one, except myself.

---

* kolobok (Russian: колобок)—a round bun in a Russian folktale

I Hear a Rattle of Bones

"I hear a rattle of bones—or are they sticks?
What is this rattle, this distant noise
or is something wrong with my hearing?
It's nothing, they tell me, nothing at all,
It's just a train passing, a train full of heavy furniture.
If it's furniture, then why does it have this smell,
like the stench of human flesh,
rotten flesh, and the sound of bones,
bone hitting bone, like a soundtrack
of a bad horror movie shown on Halloween.
So who does the bell toll for this time, tell me?"

"Excuse me, ma'am, I don't hear any bell.
I only hear three silver bells tinkling sweetly."

"Listen better, young fool, for it tolls for thee."

"I don't know what you mean by 'thee,' ma'am.
I don't hear any bell, or a rattle of, as you call them, 'bones.'"

"Listen better, fool, for it tolls for thee."

"Don't scare me, ma'am, I'm a good boy.
I go to bed at nine, and I sleep very well.
Your strange words are giving me nightmares.
I don't want scary stories about the past, ma'am.
I don't want to hear the rattle, as you say, of bones.
I want to believe in a kind God who gives me his blessing,
and if you wish to go on about the rattle of bones, ma'am,
can't you go somewhere else, somewhere far away?"

"I hear a rattle of ...."

"Just shut up now! It's a train full of furniture, as I said.
Go away now! Just go far far away!"

"Another thing about a war..."

Another thing about a war
(besides the thing we all know,
the one about killing)
is that, once it begins,
you have no right to talk about small things,
such as koalas, trees, melting ice, poems, and paintings,
which, when you think about it,
are worth talking about more than any war.

Words

Words, you lay in my hand like pebbles,
round and peaceful.
But sounds of war came from far away,
and the sea took away the pebbles,
and now my hand is empty of words

A Conversation with a Bomb

A bomb said to a city:
"I'm falling."
The city asked:
"Whose side are you on?"
The bomb said:
"I take no sides. I'm falling."
The city said:
"Look around you."
The bomb said:
"Too late."
The city did not say anything.

Upon Seeing a Portrait of Genrikh Yagoda* on a Wall in a Moscow Police Station

Drawn and redrawn
so many times over,
caught and let go
so many times
that even they lost count;
so many times renamed,
so many slogans abandoned,
so many limbs bound and loosed,
so many bullets in so many backs of heads,
so many bodies in so many mass graves,
so many feet that did not run away,
so many mouths that did not speak,
so many inheritors of what can't be described,
so many grandchildren of victims
so many grandchildren of perpetrators
that even the memory of whose grandfather
was a victim, and whose, a perpetrator,
has been lost.

---

* Genrikh Grigoryevich Yagoda was a Soviet secret police official who served as director of the NKVD the Soviet Union's security and intelligence agency, from 1934 to 1936. Under Stalin, Yagoda supervised the arrests, show trials, and executions of countless innocent people.

Babi Yar

Where's your good-for-nothing sister, said his mother.
Today we are going to die together, as a family.
Don't you hear, the Krauts are knocking at the door again!
Collect yourself quickly, and why take so many books.
Where you're going, you'll manage without them.
You're always the last one, son, said his mother.
Time to get ready, and now you want to sleep!
You'll have a good sleep where we're going to lie down together.
Rather than slip books in your bag, find your sister.
Well, what a fool you are, indeed, what station?
There's your sister, found at last, the whole family lies here together.
And the one who led their column to slaughter
lived to collect his pension, to have grandchildren
and even great-grandchildren, all of whom are so sensitive,
they'd be hurt by talk about some sort of forest,
so what, aren't there all kinds of forests in the world,
so what, no one is going to rise from there,
so don't talk about how he aimed for the mother,
and about how her youngest boy wanted to sleep,
and how his body fell on the mother's, and how the books
and some chalk dropped from his hand onto the bodies . . .
Keep silent, why tell the grandson about that forest.

My Father's Medals

Spirit of memory,
tempted by pride,
by a display of medals
on an old man's jacket
—we saw, we died, we won—
not exactly the old "veni vidi vici";
no need to tempt mortality
with tales of heroic feats,
as you, too, are mortal,
and your time shall come.
My father, a veteran,
never showed off his medals.
I saw them only once,
when I was six or seven,
"Show me!" I insisted.
He showed me an old cardboard box
with several dusty medals,
two or three or four,
I don't remember exactly;
he never took them out of that box,
and when we left our Soviet motherland forever,
it remained on a windowsill
of our Moscow apartment,
together with my mother's PhD dissertation,
(there were only so many—or so few—
things you could take with you in those days,
and I, a silly child, refused to leave
without my childhood paintings,
so they took my paintings and books and photographs,
all of these were given to a Dutch consul,
as you couldn't take certain things with you
in those early days when Soviet Jews

were exchanged for American grain),
that's how my childhood paintings
won over the medals.

("What use is pride
after twenty members of your family
are slaughtered like cattle?")

Pride of a survivor is fiction,
my father said,
and he agreed with Primo Levy,
maybe that's why he never showed his medals,
never even mentioned he was a veteran,
never joined any parade
or a veterans' group;
he didn't kill himself like Primo Levy,
he didn't talk about the war,
yet his thoughts were passed on to me
like a silent memory,
and maybe that's why sometimes I remember
things I never lived through myself.

Leap into the Air

Stone words hard to yield,
smooth as the moon washed of night,
shape me into a weapon no one can see
except with the eyes of the bones.
Words tight as skin in a fleshless space,
worn thin in a cage of promise,
design fast a leap into the air
no man can follow, see, or stop
with the scared silk of nightly kisses
or daily prayers in his expectant hand.

Pebbles

Pressed in her hand, pebbles
leap out of their clustered past,
scattering skyward the warmth
of her child-pink palm; swiftly
they fall an assigned pond—
to remember the air made visible
in the many wings of her eyes,
the rehearsal of flight made audible
in her ripening lips,
and the body of time underneath her skin,
still, yet living.

Substance Scattered in Bristling Air

Watch the bristling hills
hide in the unseen shape
of the clouds' narrowing body
restrained by nothing save
the sky, night after night,
bent on self-preservation:
substance scattered in twisted air.
Watch the wrung clouds stagger
down to where the sands drift,
the seas hum, the rocks huddle,
where, entangled in sterile crags,
air reclaims its pride.

Perched Between Pities

Perched between Pities,
kiss their hands
soiled with dogwood,
veined like a leaf.
Kiss faces of kinship
of the earth—and the heart
flowing sleep-swift,
to the shy, the sad ones
whose eyes no other eyes
seek; whose words
freeze in unheeding air.
Go to them; see:
neck-deep in pity,
your awed self, sealed.

Count Line Against Poise

Count line against poise
of unscarred days' stillness,
breeze soft and evasive,
shaping dance of the sea
under hushed skies, bearing
no grudge against those
who, weary of sly weapons,
use words pronged as pikes—
agile lies, scattering
men to shadow,
spirit—to further ridges.

How Slowly the Seagulls Circle

See how slowly the seagulls circle,
their wings flapping sleepily
over the red clay by the lake,
the same clay from which the Greeks
molded their narrow vases
with patterns from the lives of the gods
(those who own the secret of death,
turned out to be subject to it)—
gods made from red clay
at the lake of sleepily circling birds.

Acknowledgments

Some of these poems first appeared in *WordCityLit, Another Chicago Magazine, Vox Populi, Carmina Magazine, The Fictional Café, Sreda* (Russia), *The Café Review, Atunis Poetry, Pratik, Third Wednesday Magazine, Unlikely Stories, Live Encounters, Eratio, Trafika Europe, Human Rights Festival, Literary Yard, Ekphrastic Review, Kelp Journal, The Rutherford Red Wheelbarrow, Why Nicht?, Alea, Modern Poetry Review, Empirical, The Classical Outlook,* and *Gods and Mortals: Modern Poems on Classical Myths,* an Oxford University Press anthology.

About the Author

Nina Kossman's ten books include three volumes of poetry, two volumes of short prose in Russian and one in English, an anthology she edited for Oxford University Press, two volumes of translations of Marina Tsvetaeva's poetry, and a novel. Her English-language work has appeared in over ninety magazines and anthologies and has been translated into twelve languages. Her plays have been produced in the US, the UK, and Australia. Her work in her native language, Russian, was published in Russian-language literary magazines. She received grants from the Onassis Foundation, the Foundation for Hellenic Culture, a NEA fellowship, and the UNESCO/PEN Short Story Award. She lives in New York where she edits *East West Literary Forum*, a bilingual literary journal.

www.ingramcontent.com/pod-product-compliance
Lightning Source LLC
Chambersburg PA
CBHW020205090426
42734CB00008B/942